FTCE

Business Education Practice Questions

Dear Future Exam Success Story

First of all, **THANK YOU** for purchasing Mometrix study materials!

Second, congratulations! You are one of the few determined test-takers who are committed to doing whatever it takes to excel on your exam. **You have come to the right place.** We developed these practice tests with one goal in mind: to deliver you the best possible approximation of the questions you will see on test day.

Standardized testing is one of the biggest obstacles on your road to success, which only increases the importance of doing well in the high-pressure, high-stakes environment of test day. Your results on this test could have a significant impact on your future, and these practice tests will give you the repetitions you need to build your familiarity and confidence with the test content and format to help you achieve your full potential on test day.

Your success is our success

We would love to hear from you! If you would like to share the story of your exam success or if you have any questions or comments in regard to our products, please contact us at **800-673-8175** or **support@mometrix.com**.

Thanks again for your business and we wish you continued success!

Sincerely,
The Mometrix Test Preparation Team

Printed in the United States of America

Table of Contents

Practice Test #1

1. A manufacturer of high-end baby equipment needs to increase market share. They have developed a new product that has similar features to their higher-end model, but it is made with lower quality materials, creating a less expensive product. Their goal is to expand their clientele into the middle-class market. On which of the following forms of market segmentation is the company likely focusing?

a. Geographic
b. Demographic
c. Psychographic
d. Behavioral

2. Which approach to assessment offers the strongest chance of quantifying what a student has learned?

a. Multiple choice tests
b. Essay questions
c. Combining several methods
d. Tests using a simple question-and-answer format

3. Which of the following is the best technique for answering the following question in a job interview:

"What is your greatest weakness?"

a. Be as honest as possible; you will build trust with the interviewer.
b. Think of a weakness that you can turn into a strength.
c. Research a response in advance, regardless if it relates to you.
d. Try to guess what the interviewer would want to hear.

4. A market in which product availability exceeds demand is called a:

a. Free market
b. Seller's market
c. Buyer's market
d. Black market

5. Research indicates that people are most satisfied with careers that match their personalities. ____________________________ classifies personal interests and work environments to highlight aspects that are in common.

a. Career counseling
b. A personality questionnaire
c. A career assessment
d. Online research

Refer to the following for questions 6–7:

You are the advisor for the senior trip committee. The officers want to poll the class to determine where most students want to go, how much they are willing to spend, and other important planning questions. As a business teacher, you suggest that the students should create a webpage to share important details and to receive input from the other students. Before students start on the webpage, you give them a lesson on the proper netiquette to follow when creating the site.

6. What type of web design feature will most likely be used to poll the students?

a. Forms
b. Cards
c. Surveys
d. Feedback

7. Which of the following should NOT be included in the lesson on netiquette?

a. Avoid off-topic posting.
b. Share with discretion and use respectful language.
c. Don't type in all caps.
d. Netiquette doesn't apply to text messaging.

8. Which of these statements accurately reflects recommended practices for giving students learning goals and feedback?

a. Learning goals for students should be unrelated to their personal goals.
b. Contracts are good ways to define goals and grades for reaching them.
c. Teachers should give students general, delayed, and positive feedback.
d. Teachers should be the only ones who lead student feedback sessions.

9. A business education teacher wants to evaluate her program in terms of how well graduates are prepared for the workforce. Which of the following strategies would be most likely to provide the best data to answer this question?

a. Setting up an advisory committee of local employers to gather feedback on graduates' performance in the workplace
b. Asking students to complete internships with local employers
c. Conducting a survey of recent graduates to see if they were able to find jobs with local employers
d. Asking the business professors at a local community college to provide feedback

10. What is the biggest challenge or risk associated with conducting an employee satisfaction survey?

a. Skewed results because only the most satisfied employees respond
b. The potential for employees to not be truthful in their responses
c. The potential for the responses to not be anonymous
d. No employer follow-through on the results gathered from employees

11. Which is NOT an input device?

a. Mouse and keyboard
b. Memory card
c. Webcam
d. Microphone

12. Which is the set of principles, standards, and procedures that are used when compiling financial information for US corporations?

a. FASB
b. GARP
c. IFRS
d. GAAP

Refer to the following for question 13:

A high school student has expressed interest in starting her own auto repair business after graduating from high school. She asks you if there are any work-based learning opportunities where she could work in an existing auto repair business for a short time to gather experience and learn more about the industry.

13. Which opportunity should you suggest to this student?

a. Job shadowing
b. Internships
c. Mentorships
d. Co-ops

14. Which part of an organization's structure relates to the sequence of work operations by a person or a group?

a. Service provision
b. Team organization
c. Automation
d. Workflow

15. Which of the following assignments would be most helpful for a high school engineering class to improve their understanding of the responsibilities and experience in the workplace?

a. An authentic practice job interview by business owners within the community
b. A brief, daily discussion of an ethics-focused scenario in the classroom
c. A portfolio including a sales call, a presentation, and written professional goals
d. A graded policy requiring students to dress professionally once a week

16. Jim runs a company that fabricates small metal components that are used by other companies to make various types of mechanical parts. It is imperative that these parts are created with precision to exact specifications; otherwise, the components used may not fit or could cause malfunctions. Efficiency is essential, as profit margins are low, and waste can quickly damage the bottom line. Every employee at Jim's company shares his regard for customer satisfaction and efficient operations, from sales, to finance, to the CNC machine operators, and they aim for continually improving the customer experience. These shared values have created much success for the company. What type of operations management process is Jim likely implementing in his company?

a. Total quality management
b. Enterprise resource planning
c. Strategic planning
d. Operational design

17. What is a disadvantage of using rubrics as assessment tools?

a. Learning objectives, tasks, guidance, and criteria are combined.
b. Performance levels are not as precise as grades or percentages.
c. They afford greater brevity in definition, guidance, assessment.
d. Rubrics are more concise yet offer more clarity than other tools.

18. What is the field of study that focuses on the relationships between people, technology, and organizations for the purpose of more efficient managerial decision-making?

a. Demographics
b. Sociology
c. Operations management
d. Management information systems

19. What is the concept of international law that gives individual countries the option to refuse to sign an international treaty?

a. Comity of nations
b. Sovereignty of states
c. Amicus curiae
d. Sovereign succession

20. What is the most common mode of entry into a foreign market?

a. Licensing
b. Exporting
c. Franchising
d. Partnering with a local entity

21. Which of the following is NOT a benefit of written communication?

a. Provides a paper trail
b. Gives the author time to think about what they want to say
c. Allows the communicator to fully express their thoughts without interruption
d. Prevents confusion due to a lack of tone

22. Choose the list below that best describes the most important contents of a resume:

a. Salary requirements, relevant work experience, educational attainment, objective
b. Contact information, grade point average, relevant work experience, objective
c. References, objective, educational attainment, salary requirements
d. Contact information, objective, educational attainment, relevant work experience

23. Which of the following would violate federal child labor regulations?

a. Hiring your own child to work in your small business if the child is under 14
b. Employing someone under 14 as a newspaper carrier
c. Employing someone under 18 in a job deemed hazardous
d. Employing anyone under 18 as a babysitter

24. Stan owns and operates a printing shop which has been open for two years. The shop has been mostly successful, but Stan is barely breaking even at the end of the fiscal year. He believes that a new, top-of-the-line printer will bring in new clientele and greatly increase his revenue. He needs to raise the capital required to purchase the new printer. Which of the following would be the most likely source of capital to pay for the new printer?

a. Bank loan
b. Venture capitalist
c. Crowdfunding
d. Bootstrapping

25. A manager gives a floor worker free reign to implement a new organization system that helps to cycle out old stock right before new stock arrives. She notices over the next few weeks that the employee's performance in other areas improves as well. What is the motivational theory that suggests the employee will be more successful when they are challenged to grow professionally based on their skills and abilities?

a. Piaget's cognitive stages
b. Locke's goal-setting theory
c. McClelland's achievement motivation theory
d. Maslow's hierarchy of needs

26. When a consumer purchases a new mattress from a manufacturer, they have the right to expect that mattress to meet safety standards and to have the features the manufacturer claims it has, even if there is no explicit promise made. What form of contract does this represent?

a. Express contract
b. Written contract
c. Implied in-law contract
d. Implied in-fact contract

27. When itemizing deductions on a federal tax return, an individual taxpayer may be able to deduct all but which of the following?

a. Interest paid on a mortgage
b. Charitable donations
c. Losses from theft
d. Life insurance premiums

28. Ben is a database administrator at the local school district. One of the teachers in the district has recently been promoted to assistant principal. In this new position, she will need to be able to access more secure student information that she was not privy to as a teacher. What settings does Ben need to change for her?

a. Elevate security clearances
b. Increase user permissions
c. Modify role-based access controls
d. Change from user to administrator

29. Which of the following best describes Congress' purpose in setting up Freddie Mac in 1970?

a. Expanding opportunities for home ownership
b. Deregulating the credit market
c. Improving regulation of the Internet
d. Creating a place for small businesses to get loans

30. Which is the most common format for a formal business letter?

a. Block style
b. Modified block
c. Indented block
d. Semi-block

31. What is the name of the document that guides a company's day-to-day operations and financial decisions?

a. Financial report
b. Business plan
c. Loan application
d. Strategic plan

32. Which term refers to the use of cable, telephone, or other broadcasting systems (wired or wireless) to transmit information over a distance?

a. Digital signaling
b. Media networking
c. Telecommunications
d. Input and output devices

33. Which pay structure is most commonly associated with people working in sales?

a. Commission
b. Salary
c. Hourly
d. Base plus tips

34. Which of the following is a common expert recommendation that allows teachers to address problematic student behaviors?

a. Teachers cannot and should not try to view school through students' eyes.
b. Teachers' own experiences with teachers, either good or bad, are irrelevant.
c. Teachers should list words that describe their feelings when interacting with teachers/supervisors and what evoked them.
d. Teachers should focus on their perceptions of students but not vice versa.

35. An engineer at an automobile manufacturer discovers a potential issue with the engines of the latest model of cars being produced. The flaw could cause the engine to overheat and catch fire. The engineer brings this issue to the attention of management, but they decide that the likelihood of the engine catching fire is low enough that it does not justify the expense of repairing the cars already produced. However, they agree to adjust the engines on all cars being produced going forward. Which of the following consumer rights is this company failing to meet?

a. Access to information
b. Marketing transparency
c. Product liability
d. Consumer guarantee

36. A successful manager will be able to effectively delegate:

a. Responsibility
b. Accountability
c. Authority
d. Ability

37. How do banks and lenders use credit scores to determine creditworthiness?

a. They show how much money the consumer has available to cover the risk
b. They provide recent historical data of the consumer's use of credit
c. It is an insurance policy if the consumer defaults on a debt
d. They document the consumer's use of credit over the span of their lifetime

38. The Internet is an example of what type of network?

a. LAN
b. WAN
c. PAN
d. MAN

39. A careers course teacher has assigned a final cumulative assignment that must include a title page, cover letter, resume, work samples, and references. Which of the following best describes the assignment?

a. Career portfolio
b. Job application
c. Interview packet
d. Biography

40. Which choice below is NOT a characteristic of the sole proprietorship form of business ownership?

a. The owner has flexibility with how the business is operated.
b. It is the most common form of business ownership.
c. Establishing a sole proprietorship is costly and complex.
d. The owner is personally liable for all business obligations.

41. Which of the following steps of the buying decision process should a business focus on in order to increase long-term market share?

a. Adoption
b. Evaluation
c. Loyalty
d. Interest

42. A consumer's credit score is usually a factor in all but which of the following transactions?

a. Buying a car
b. Buying a home
c. Getting a personal loan
d. Opening a bank account

43. The primary objective of ____ accounting is to provide accounting data for the purpose of making business decisions, such as making big purchases, financial forecasting, and having a general understanding of how well a business is performing.

a. government
b. forensic
c. financial
d. managerial

44. Which of these federal pieces of legislation is the country's main education law for all public schools and specifies that career and technical education be included in a well-rounded education?

a. No Child Left Behind Act
b. Workforce Innovation and Opportunity Act
c. Individuals with Disabilities Education Act
d. Every Student Succeeds Act

45. Language barriers, cultural differences, and nonverbal communication norms are all potential causes of communication issues that can arise when doing business ____.

a. Locally
b. With governments
c. Internationally
d. Between states

46. What is the name given to companies who produce goods and/or deliver services in more than one country?

a. Global corporations
b. Cross-border entities
c. Multinational enterprises
d. Import/export companies

47. Which of the following would benefit most from being organized with a spreadsheet database?

a. A student event calendar
b. Storing student scores on assignments
c. A simple rubric for scoring assignments
d. A set of classroom rules meant to be printed

48. Which of the following lists contains only types of computer software?

a. Internet, Microsoft Office, Quicken
b. Motherboard, Quicken, Excel
c. Quicken, Peoplesoft, Microsoft Office
d. Monitor, Mouse, Keyboard

49. You are in a department meeting, and your department chair is discussing the recent formalized test scores the school received. He explains that last year's 11th graders in the district scored very low on several standards, some of which should be covered in more than one course offered by your department. How can you and your colleagues work together to determine the gaps in instruction to ensure future students learn these important standards?

a. Ask administration to review course descriptions to determine who should be responsible for teaching those standards.
b. Prepare a list of reasons why these standards are not covered in any of your courses.
c. Compare formative test scores across several courses to determine which students seem to be struggling the most, and offer them additional instructional support.
d. Review curriculum maps of related courses with the other members of the department to see if/when the standards are covered.

50. What is the term for the correct or acceptable way to communicate on the internet?

a. Netiquette
b. Grammarly
c. Common Courtesy
d. Online Protocol

51. Verbal harassment, gossip, exclusion, and aggression are examples of

a. Coping skills
b. Workplace conflict
c. Compromise
d. Management meetings

52. Corporation X, the largest oil refiner in the US, wants to purchase Corporation Y, the only other oil refiner in the US. This situation may be of concern to the government because:

a. It may violate environmental laws.
b. It may constitute a violation of antitrust laws.
c. It could violate labor laws by reducing employees' choice of employers.
d. It could constitute a pyramid scheme.

53. How can teachers best help students prepare for unexpected changes in the workplace?

a. Teachers should encourage students to only study skills for specific careers to save time and get ahead in their desired industries.
b. Teachers should teach transferable and generic skills that can be applied to multiple careers.
c. Teachers should urge students to go to trade schools instead of traditional four-year universities, as traditional degrees are over-saturated and no longer valuable.
d. Teachers should not generally take responsibility for students' career choices.

54. When designing a website for an online business, the web developer would include a site map in order to:

a. Give website users directions to the business.
b. Provide website users with a list of links to all of the pages on the website.
c. Convince website users that it is safe to purchase products from the website.
d. Help website users decide which products to buy from the website.

55. Which of the following is NOT true regarding sexual harassment regulations?

a. Hostile environment harassment must be pervasive or severe to be considered a violation.
b. Sexual harassment is separated into quid pro quo and hostile environment cases.
c. Employees who voice discomfort may request that the environment be changed.
d. Victims must suffer loss to be considered a violation.

56. Which one of these actions is NOT included in consumer protection laws?

a. Checking an organization's reputation
b. Enforcing antitrust regulations
c. Regulating bill collectors
d. Preventing sellers from fraudulent tactics

57. Which of these would NOT be a step in applying for a job?

a. Searching for jobs and researching companies
b. Completing employer assessments
c. Following up after an interview
d. Onboarding

58. In designing a group project, Mr. Aaron wants to implement an assessment system that provides incentives for all students to contribute equally to the project and that is fair to students in cases where certain group members contribute more than others. Which of the following strategies would be most effective in helping him achieve this objective?

a. Giving all students in the group the opportunity to confidentially rate the contributions of their fellow group members and giving lower grades to students who are rated lower by the members of their group
b. Giving all students in the group the same grade so that they'll be motivated to monitor one another's contributions and exercise teamwork skills
c. Asking students to submit a report detailing exactly what their contribution was to the project and to provide a self-evaluation of the value of their own contribution
d. Grading the projects using a pass/fail system, since it is very difficult to equitably grade group projects

59. A phrase that is associated with a particular product would be protected by which of the following?

a. Trademark law
b. Patent law
c. Copyright law
d. Both A and C

60. Which of the following activities would most effectively and comprehensively assess students' mastery of learning objectives for a unit about small business?

a. Asking students to create and market a new invention
b. Asking students to design and implement a community service project
c. Requiring students to complete an internship or externship
d. Having students write and present a business plan

61. What is the federal retirement program that is funded through payroll deductions?

a. 401(k) plans
b. IRAs
c. Social Security
d. Pension plans

62. GDP measures a country's:

a. Employment level
b. Education level
c. Total economic output
d. Wage levels

63. Amanda uses a word processor to write company memos, send invoices, and write letters. Her company requires that she uses the corporate logo and other specific information on each letter. She finds these extra steps to be time consuming and inefficient. Which function could Amanda use to reduce the number of steps involved in this process?

a. Format painter
b. Macros
c. Clipboard
d. Mail merge

64. Comprehensive car insurance typically covers:

a. Damage the insured does to the property of others while driving the insured vehicle
b. Medical expenses others incur as a result of a collision with the insured vehicle
c. Damage done to the insured's vehicle by a vandal
d. All of the above

65. A teacher who is also a student organization advisor should do which of the following?

a. Be a sounding board, mentor members with individual and group issues, and guide the students in the organization to develop goals and delegate tasks.
b. Establish group policies and procedures, maintain accurate and consistent records, and run all organization meetings.
c. Be responsible for recruiting new members, influence the decisions of the organization leaders, and enforce disciplinary action when needed.
d. Set long-term goals for the organization, assign roles for individual projects, and always model ethical behavior.

66. Which of the following does NOT reflect a role of the Small Business Administration?

a. It helps create jobs and reduce unemployment.
b. It provides access to capital for small business owners.
c. It provides government advocacy for small business owners.
d. It provides fee-based entrepreneurial development.

67. Which type of intellectual property is the familiar sign that consumers easily recognize and connect to a brand?

a. Patents
b. Trademarks
c. Copyrights
d. Trade secrets

68. An example of ____ communication style is using I-statements.

a. Aggressive
b. Assertive
c. Passive
d. Passive-aggressive

69. Accounts receivable are:

a. Fixed assets
b. Fixed liabilities
c. Current assets
d. Current liabilities

70. Which of the following sets the rules for how computers and computer networks (known collectively as the internet) communicate with each other?

a. Broadband access
b. Internet protocol
c. Internet service providers
d. Virtual private networks

71. You are serving as a cooperating teacher for a college student preparing to complete her requirements to earn a teaching certificate. The student asks you for suggestions on how to network with other teachers, find mentor teachers during her first few years of teaching, and help her with continuing education hours for personal and professional growth. Which of the following would be the best advice for the student?

a. Stay in touch with her student cohort from her current classes.
b. Ask a veteran teacher to be her mentor.
c. Join a professional association, such as the National Business Education Association.
d. Suggest she joins teacher groups on social media.

72. Which of the following is the primary function of a product manager?

a. Preparing product materials for sales representatives
b. Planning and controlling long-range plans for specific products
c. Managing and overseeing the training of field representatives
d. Allocating resources to various members of the supply chain

73. Which of the following is NOT considered a domestic economic advantage of global trade?

a. Global trade provides raw materials to countries that otherwise would not have access.
b. Global trade reduces costs of production, therefore also reducing prices for consumers.
c. Global trade creates mutual economic growth between trading nations.
d. Global trade allows for imports on some goods, such as agriculture, much cheaper than buying domestically.

74. Which of the following entrepreneur factors is most likely to cause the failure of a small business due to inadequate day-to-day management?

a. Lack of drive and passion
b. Lack of financial knowledge
c. Lack of experience in operations management
d. Lack of community support

75. Which of the following list contains ONLY examples of soft skills?

a. Adaptable, mathematical, problem-solver
b. Bilingual, creative, intelligent
c. Cooperative, persuasive, musical ability
d. Strong work ethic, time management skills, communication skills

76. Regarding Mintzberg's managerial roles, which of the following is NOT included in the interpersonal category of roles?

a. Spokesperson
b. Figurehead
c. Leader
d. Liaison

77. The Equal Employment Opportunity Commission (EEOC) is responsible for enforcing all but which of the following laws?

a. Civil Rights Act of 1964
b. Equal Pay Act
c. Clean Air Act
d. Americans with Disabilities Act

78. Which business discipline is defined as the practice that includes researching, identifying, and satisfying consumer needs and wants?

a. Marketing
b. Organizational behavior
c. Communication
d. Sales management

79. What is the most efficient way to send a large group of addresses a copy of an email while keeping each email address private?

a. Adding everyone in a cc
b. Forwarding it to everyone on the list
c. Adding everyone in a bcc
d. Sending each recipient a separate email

80. Owners' equity is composed of:

a. The personal net worth of the owners plus the amount of their initial investment in the business
b. The amount of the owners' initial investment in the business
c. The owners' unclaimed profits from the business' operation
d. Both B and C

Answer Key and Explanations for Test #1

1. B: Demographic market segmentation is the method of grouping consumers by variables such as age, gender, education, family size, or income. This company is trying to expand outside of their normal clientele, likely upper-class individuals and families with substantial disposable income. Making an affordable model under their desirable label allows them to expand into the middle-class segment with less disposable income, requiring the price to be reduced on the new product.

2. C: Some students perform better on tests, while others do better with papers or other projects. Just as students learn in a variety of ways, their talents for expressing what they have learned also varies widely. A teacher that evaluates students based on a wide variety of tasks will come away with a much more complete picture of each student's strengths and weaknesses.

3. B: Think of a weakness that you can turn into a strength. One example is, "I struggle to ask for help when I need it." This is a response that can be turned into a strength. "I am an independent and hard worker, and sometimes I do not realize when I need to ask for help. I work hard to complete a task on my own, but I am working on asking for help when needed."

4. C: A market in which product availability is greater than product demand is called a buyer's market, because when supply (product availability) exceeds demand, the prices paid by buyers decrease. This decrease in prices benefits the buyer of a product and decreases the seller's profits.

5. C: Career assessments (many of which can be taken online at no cost) help individuals understand the classification of various personality traits and the impact of different careers and work environments on those personality traits. These assessments help individuals make better informed career choices. Holland Code is one popular system used to classify work personalities.

6. A: A web design form is a type of page that allows the user to input information, which can be collected and stored for the owner of the web page to view. The types of responses you can use in a web design form are drop-downs, short response, paragraph response, multiple choice, multiple select, and others.

7. D: In addition to avoiding off-topic posting, sharing with discretion, and not typing in all caps (considered "yelling"), here are other common netiquette guidelines: respond to emails promptly, do not attach large files, respect others' privacy, fact-check before reposting, and be careful with abbreviations. Netiquette does include emails and text messages.

8. B: One recommended way for defining student learning goals and what grades they will receive for meeting those goals is for teachers and students to write and sign contracts agreeing to goal and grade terms. Experts say student learning goals should be compatible with student personal goals, not unrelated (a). They note it is important for teachers to give students specific, timely, and corrective feedback (c). They also recommend that teachers invite students to lead feedback sessions (d).

9. A: The best way for a business education teacher to evaluate her program in terms of how well graduates are prepared for the workforce would be to consult with local business leaders to find out where graduates have room for improvement. Asking students to complete internships would help prepare students for the workforce, but it would not provide the necessary feedback on students' preparedness. Surveying recent graduates would be useful, but it would provide less direct and detailed information about their performance in the workforce. Last, community college professors would be more familiar with students' performance in college courses than their performance in the workplace.

10. D: The biggest organizational risk when conducting an employee satisfaction survey is the potential for not taking any action based on the findings of the survey. This may backfire and create ill will among employees instead of the intended result of boosting morale or making people feel heard.

11. B: Input devices are used to enter information into the system or to control operations. They include keyboards, mice (or touchpads on a laptop), webcams, and microphones. Removable media, such as flash drives and memory cards, are a way to transfer data from one computer to another.

12. D: Generally accepted accounting principles (GAAP) are issued by the Financial Accounting Standards Board (FASB) and are used when preparing financial information. International Financial Reporting Standards (IFRS) are used by more than 100 nations, including European countries. The purpose of GAAP is to provide consistent, clear, and easily comparable financial information for its users.

13. B: Work-based learning combines the classroom with real-world opportunities, and the sponsoring company is able to determine if the student may be a good employee candidate. Internships provide job experience that allows students to put into practice skills they have been learning in school. Job shadowing provides the opportunity for a new employee to observe an employee performing a specific job. Mentorships foster relationships between students and business professionals. Typically, the mentor serves as a role model, provides information about careers, and often can introduce students to other professionals for potential jobs. Cooperative education (often called a co-op) allows students to alternate time in the classroom with time in the workplace. Compared to internships, co-ops usually last longer and are often tied into a college course of study.

14. D: Workflow is the sequence of work as it moves from start to completion. Each step includes input (materials needed), transformation to the input, and output (what is produced during the transformation). A workflow diagram is often used to illustrate the steps and the workers involved.

15. C: Each of these assignments reflects workforce skills, but option C would best improve their understanding of the actual experience and responsibilities they can expect in the workplace. An interview would be useful for improving understanding of the pre-hire experience but not the workplace. Discussions about ethics concepts are helpful, but ethical decision-making does not comprise the full workplace experience. Dressing well for a job can be important; however, requiring students to dress professionally at school does not yield much varied experience for the student, and it may be difficult to implement or unreasonable to ask of students on a weekly basis.

16. A: Total quality management (TQM) involves continually improving the customer experience while minimizing errors and waste. TQM is focused on high efficiency without losing sight of the most important element of the business process: the consumer. For TQM to be fully integrated, all members of an organization must be fully committed at all levels of operation. Jim is not only committed to TQM, but he has engaged his staff to be just as dedicated.

17. B: The fact that rubrics combine learning objectives, tasks, guidance to students for performing those tasks, and criteria (A) for evaluating student task performance is an advantage they have as assessment tools. Rubrics use a combined set of criteria to try to make an objective assessment of something that is more subjective, such as a performance or presentation. A rubric is very helpful for grounding the grading of a variety of work that students can turn in, but it still is not as objective as something that uses standard, calculated grades. The fact that the performance levels teachers assign are not as precise as number or letter grades or percentages (B) is a disadvantage. The fact that they are brief in nature (C) is an advantage for both students and teachers. The fact that they are both more concise and clearer than many other assessment tools (D) is another advantage.

18. D: Management information systems is the study of the relationship between people, technology, and organizations. The information derived from these studies can help managers determine the most efficient way to allocate resources. It can also help determine what new technologies can help make people's lives easier.

19. B: Sovereignty of states allows individual countries the right to choose whether to sign or not sign an international treaty on behalf of all those living within their nations' borders. Other countries do not have the right to interfere with the decisions of others, but they may put political or economic pressure on them to force their decision.

20. B: Exporting allows a company to find a distributor in another country to sell its products directly to consumers. Although the business will need to analyze transportation costs and related tariffs, money is saved because there is no direct investment in manufacturing. Other modes of entry include licensing, franchising, setting up wholly owned subsidiaries, establishing joint ventures, and partnering with a local entity.

21. D: Written communication has many benefits, but one thing it does not do is prevent confusion due to a lack of tone or voice. It is a common occurrence for email and text communications to be misunderstood because of the absence of nonverbal cues. However, written communication does provide a paper trail to document all messages, allows more time for the writer to consider what they want to say, and permits them the chance to communicate without interruption.

22. D: The four most important parts of a resume are the applicant's contact information, objective, educational attainment, and relevant work experience. The contact information is crucial because it allows the employer to get in touch with the applicant. The objective is important because it explains why the applicant is sending the resume and what position the applicant hopes to obtain. Educational attainment and work experience are important credentials for any job, while salary requirements and employment references are typically provided in the cover letter or upon request.

23. C: It is illegal to employ someone under 18 in a job deemed hazardous. Such jobs include mining and manufacturing. Youths aged 16 and 17 can work in any job that is not hazardous, and youths under 14 can work in certain designated jobs like newspaper delivery and babysitting. In cases where state and federal laws conflict, the law that is more protective of minors takes precedence.

24. A: The best option for funding the new printer is likely a bank loan. To be successful in accomplishing this, he will need to convince his bank that he will be able to pay off the loan by demonstrating why he thinks the new printer is going to pay off. If he cannot demonstrate this, the bank will likely decline his request for a loan. Venture capitalists generally invest in more high-growth startups, such as in the tech industry. Stan's printing shop is unlikely to be considered a high-growth, scalable business. Stan is barely breaking even each year, so it is not likely he will be able to fund the cost of the printer with his own cash (bootstrapping). Crowd funding is possible, but seems unlikely as crowd funding usually surrounds novel, experimental business or fun ideas rather than a small business in an explored market.

25. B: Locke's goal-setting theory is a theory that was developed in the 1960s that insists that specific and difficult, but reasonable, goals lead to improved performance when compared to more general, easy goals. Not only is performance expected to improve, but the motivation of affected employees also often improve as a result.

26. D: An implied in-fact contract exists when two parties enter into an agreement, such as the purchase of a mattress. The manufacturer is expected to produce a mattress that meets all advertised expectations, and the customer is expected to pay the price the manufacturer charges and to use the product as it is intended to be used.

27. D: When itemizing deductions on a federal tax return, a taxpayer may be able to deduct all of the things listed here except for life insurance premiums. Mortgage interest, losses from theft, and charitable donations are all tax-deductible under certain circumstances.

28. B: Ben would need to change her user permissions to allow access to more secure fields or pages of the database. User permissions protect personal information from those who may not need to view all details. This also protects the user in the event of an information leak; those without access to the more secure information are excluded from an investigation of a data leak.

29. A: Expanding opportunities for home ownership was Congress' primary purpose in setting up Freddie Mac. This organization was charged with increasing the availability of money for home loans by pooling mortgages together to create mortgage-backed securities.

30. A: Letters presented in block style are entirely left justified and presented in single space (except for a double space between paragraphs). This is the most common format for a formal business letter. In the modified block style, the date, the sender's return address, closing, and signature all start near the middle of the page. Semi-block format uses indentation for the paragraphs.

31. B: A business plan is a written document that details the organization's day-to-day operational goals and financial projections and provides a strategy to address them. Although often required by lenders, it is not a loan application per se. Financial reports are prepared based on what actually happened—not the goals going forward.

32. C: Examples of telecommunication networks include telephone networks, the internet, and any network that expedites the transfer of data among many users. There are three components: the transmitter that converts information into a signal, the medium that carries the signal, and the receiver that accepts the signal and converts it back to the original information.

33. A: The most common pay structure for someone working in a sales position is commission-based pay. The purpose of this type of compensation is to encourage higher sales. If structured fairly, both the employee and employer can mutually benefit from commission-based pay. The more sales or new clients the employee lands, the more money they make, and the company increases revenue.

34. C: Experts recommend that teachers imagine school through their students' eyes to understand them better, contrary to what option A suggests. Experts also recommend that teachers reflect about their own best and worst teachers/supervisors when considering students' perspectives, unlike answer B suggests. Like option C describes, experts recommend that teachers create a list of the feelings they experienced when interacting with teachers and supervisors in their own lives, along with what evoked those feelings. This is meant to gain insight into students' reactions to what teachers say and do. Contrary to what option D suggests, experts recommend that teachers should not focus on their own perceptions of students but rather try to understand how students perceive the teacher.

35. C: The automobile manufacturer failed to meet consumer rights regarding liability. If any of the engines catch fire, the manufacturer is liable for any injuries resulting from the fire and also any damage to the vehicle. Consumers have the right to rely on the products they purchase to meet minimum safety standards.

36. C: A successful manager will be able to effectively delegate authority. As a leader, the manager always retains accountability for results and ultimate responsibility for employees' actions. However, the manager must be able to delegate decision-making authority to subordinate employees in order to fulfill his or her job function. Ability (D) can be improved through training, but it cannot be automatically delegated.

37. B: A credit score is a numerical representation of a consumer's history with credit. It is based on several factors, including payment history, total debt, length of credit history, types of credit, and new credit. Typically, negative items on a credit report that affect credit scores remain for up to 7 years and are eventually removed. Lenders use the credit score to determine the risk of the consumer defaulting on the loan. The higher the credit score, the more likely a consumer will be approved for lending.

38. B: The Internet is an example of a wide area network (WAN). A WAN is a network that spans a large geographical area and connects other networks, allowing them to communicate with each other over large distances.

39. A: A career portfolio is made up of an important set of documents that outline a professional's goals, experience, education, samples of work, skills and awards, and references. This is an important collection of materials that students can use as they prepare to apply to post-secondary education or to enter the workforce after graduation.

40. C: Sole proprietorships—the most common form of business ownership—are easy to form, and there is typically very little regulation. Start-up requirements often involve simply securing a business license. The owner has flexibility with how the business is operated and is personally liable for all business obligations.

41. C: Of the six steps in the buying decision process, customer loyalty is key to long-term market share increase. While it is important to gain consumer attention and interest, as well as guide them to trial and adoption, returning customers are essential to long-term increases in market share. Not only will their continuous purchases increase profits, but they are also likely to bring more consumers with them via word of mouth.

42. D: A consumer's credit score may be considered when a consumer buys a car or home if the transaction involves a loan, and it will also be considered if an individual applies for a personal loan. However, one's credit score is not usually considered when opening a bank account, as the account holder is depositing money rather than borrowing it.

43. D: The goal of managerial accounting is to collect a business' financial data, analyze the information, and present the material in a way that makes sense to the business decision-makers. This is different than most other forms of accounting, in that the other types of accounting focus on reporting information to individuals outside of the business.

44. D: The Every Student Succeeds Act (ESSA) became law in December 2015 and replaced the No Child Left Behind Act as the primary education law. The Workforce Innovation and Opportunity Act (WIOA) helps job seekers enter the labor market. The Individuals with Disabilities Act (IDEA) is a federal law for special education.

45. C: There are many issues that can arise with international business. There can be misunderstandings when translating between businesses. Cultural differences can inadvertently lead to offending those with different expectations. Handshakes, eye contact, and other nonverbal communication differences can also cause communication problems.

46. C: Multinational enterprises (MNEs) own or conduct business in more than one country (including subsidiaries and affiliated companies), and they typically earn at least 25 percent of their revenues outside of their home country. Well-known MNEs (also called multinational corporations) include Apple, Ford, Nike, Microsoft, and Coca-Cola. Global corporations, cross-border entities, and import/export companies describe MNE operations.

47. B: Each of these could be expressed through a spreadsheet, but spreadsheet-style databases would be particularly effective in organizing student scores, since it can be used for calculating averages and keeping track of low grades or missing scores. Calendars would be best designed with a calendar making software. Classroom rules and rubrics would likely be best organized simply using a word processor software.

48. C: Quicken, PeopleSoft, and Microsoft Office are all types of computer software. Quicken is used by individuals and small businesses for basic accounting functions, PeopleSoft is used primarily by human resources professionals, and Microsoft Office is the most widely used productivity software on the market. The Internet is not a type of software because it is not a program that can be installed and run on a single computer's operating system. The monitor, mouse, motherboard, and keyboard are all hardware or equipment that is required to make software usable.

49. D: The best strategy in this situation is to review the curriculum maps of related courses with all members in the department to determine which courses are covering those standards, which courses are not being covered but should be, and how each teacher is teaching that standard. This process is not to place blame on individual teachers. Rather, this is an opportunity to learn from each other and improve instructional strategies.

50. A: Netiquette refers to the common rules of etiquette that apply while communicating over the internet. Without facial expressions or nonverbal cues, misunderstandings can happen. Netiquette attempts to discourage unwanted behavior with established social conventions. Grammarly is a software that checks grammar, spelling, and potential plagiarism. It also offers writing suggestions.

51. B: Workplaces include individuals with varying backgrounds and different expectations. Verbal harassment, gossip, exclusion, and aggression are examples of workplace conflict that can occur as a result of these differences. It is inevitable that conflicts will arise; however, it is important that these conflicts be addressed and resolved as expeditiously as possible to avoid harming the work group and the company.

52. B: This situation may constitute a violation of antitrust law. If the only two oil refiners in the US merged, this would mean that there would be only one oil refiner in the US, thus creating a monopoly. Monopolies are generally illegal because they eliminate competition that ensures fair prices for consumers.

53. B: Given the changing nature of the workplace, it is critical that students learn basic business education skills—many of which are transferable. It is also important that teachers present generic skills for students to be prepared for opportunities as they arise. While career-specific skills and knowledge are necessary, generic, transferable skills are essential for remaining flexible in the face of unexpected changes, such as unemployment.

54. B: When designing a website for an online business, the web developer would include a site map in order to provide website users with a list of links to all of the pages on the website. Site maps, also called indexes, list each webpage that is part of the website.

55. D: Sexual harassment is separated into two types: quid pro quo (this for that) cases and hostile environment cases. Victims do not need to suffer loss. Hostile environment harassment needs to be pervasive or severe to be considered a violation. Employees may be offended by any sexual conduct in the workplace, such as lewd comments, jokes, pornographic pictures, or touching. Employees who voice discomfort may request that the environment be changed. If an employer fails to correct the offensive environment, employees may press charges without needing to demonstrate physical or psychological damage.

56. A: Consumer law topics include creating a fair marketplace by enforcing regulations, regulating bill collectors, preventing sellers from fraudulent or deceptive tactics, product liability, bill collector regulation, and utility shutoffs.

57. D: Onboarding refers to the process of bringing a newly hired employee into the company. Searching for jobs, researching companies, sending a resume and cover letter, participating in an interview, completing assessments as required by the hiring company, and following up with the company are steps that summarize the job application process.

58. A: Mr. Aaron should give all students in the group the opportunity to confidentially rate the contributions of their fellow group members and give lower grades to students who are rated lower by the members of their group. This approach will give each student an incentive to contribute equally, because they can receive a lower grade if they do not contribute. This method would allow Mr. Aaron to grade fairly in cases where certain students fail to contribute.

59. A: A phrase that is associated with a particular product would be protected by trademark law. Copyright law protects creative work, while trademarks protect business-related slogans, symbols, etc., which distinguish one product from another.

60. D: The activity that would most effectively and comprehensively assess how well students have mastered learning objectives for a unit about small business would be writing and presenting a business plan. While marketing is an important aspect of running a small business, developing a business plan would more comprehensively and directly measure and reinforce students' knowledge about small businesses.

61. C: Social Security was originally created to promote financial stability for Americans and includes retirement, disability, and survivor programs. Its participation is required by law for employers and employees. Other pension plans may be employer funded.

62. C: GDP stands for gross domestic product, and it measures a country's total economic output, including goods and services, over a given period of time. Usually, GDP is reported annually.

63. B: Macros are tools used in some applications, such as in Microsoft Word or Excel, to record or program repeatable steps and perform them automatically. One example of using macros as a single command would be to automate the process of inserting the company logo and other required information without manually inputting those items. The user can assign a button or series of keystrokes that will prompt the processor to input the pre-recorded macros. Automation can be difficult to establish but helps to improve the speed and precision of complex tasks that normally take more time or lend themselves to human error.

64. C: Comprehensive insurance typically covers damage due to vandalism. Liability insurance typically covers damage done to the property of others while driving the insured vehicle and the medical expenses of people in a collision with the insured vehicle.

65. A: The teacher-advisor in a student organization has several responsibilities. Some of these responsibilities include being a sounding board to hear students' ideas and offer suggestions; mentoring members of the group, primarily in group issues, but also individual issues as appropriate; working with the students to determine the organization's goals and delegating tasks. There are many other responsibilities, but there are also things an advisor should not do. This includes essentially doing the work for the group, such as creating the policies and procedures, keeping all records, running meetings, recruitment, manipulating group leaders, etc. The advisor is there to serve as a mentor and oversee the group. The advisor should allow the students to learn leadership skills by making decisions and carrying out most of the tasks.

66. D: The Small Business Administration provides services for small business owners, such as helping provide access to capital, government advocacy, assistance with contracts, and entrepreneurial advancement. These services are provided free of charge. With extra support from the Small Business Administration, entrepreneurs are more successful running small businesses, which creates jobs and reduces unemployment.

67. B: Trademarks distinguish similar brands from one another and include the McDonald's golden arch, Apple's logo, and the Nike swoosh. Patents protect an invention from being used without the creator's permission. Copyrights protect tangible items (not the ideas) and include written work, software code, music, and drawings. Trade secrets are proprietary company information (e.g., Mrs. Fields's cookie recipe).

68. B: Assertive communicators are able to effectively express their thoughts and opinions. Using I-statements allows an individual to clearly convey their meaning without offending others (aggressive) and without being self-conscious (passive) or sarcastic (passive-aggressive). An example of an I-statement is, "I appreciate when you give me your full attention while I am speaking in the meeting."

69. C: Accounts receivable are current assets, also known as short-term assets. This term refers to open accounts that are not yet due and those that are already due or overdue but which have not yet been paid. For example, if a landscaping company mows Anna's lawn today and the company sends her a bill for the service that is due one month later, then Anna's account would be in "account receivable" status until the due date.

70. B: The internet protocol (IP) allows data to be sent from one computer to another and defines how packets are addressed and routed. Broadband access refers to the technologies that allow access to the internet, and internet service providers (ISPs) sell the access and other services. Virtual private networks use virtualization to extend private networks across a public network, such as the internet.

71. C: While all of these suggestions are generally good practice, the best choice would be to suggest that the student join a professional association for teachers in her content specialty. Staying in touch with others from her educational cohort can be helpful, especially for networking, but they cannot offer opportunities for continuing education. Veteran teachers are an invaluable resource for guidance and may be able to help with networking, but they also do not typically offer as many opportunities for continuing education. Teacher groups on social media can also be beneficial, but there can also be misinformation in those groups. Additionally, they don't usually offer much in the way of immediate networking (unless they are local to the teacher), and they also do not offer structured educational opportunities.

72. B: Product managers, or brand managers, are the center of the marketing department in most consumer and business product firms. The product manager plans, implements, and controls the annual plans related to products for which he or she is responsible, so choice B is the best answer. Choice A is incorrect because preparing materials for sales representatives would be a job for the sales support staff. Managing field representatives would be a task for a sales force manager, so choice C is wrong. Distributing resources to suppliers is too narrow of a task for the product manager, so choice D is wrong.

73. D: While it is true that importing certain goods, such as agriculture, can be cost effective, the result of these transactions is often detrimental to domestic producers. US farmers often cannot compete with the lost costs of imported produce. Closing domestic farms has a negative impact on the economy and GDP.

74. C: Many entrepreneurs do not have the knowledge of or experience in operating and managing a business. They often want to complete all responsibilities of operating the business rather than delegating any of the responsibilities to those better suited and knowledgeable.

75. D: Soft skills are the personal aptitudes that demonstrate a person's ability to work with others or generally adapt to situations in a job. Hard skills are measurable and are usually learned with education or training. For example, hard skills mixed into the other choices include mathematics, bilingualism, and musical ability. These are considered hard-skills because they involve some sort of specific, technical skill that may apply to the job directly in a technical way. Soft skills are usually tied to a person's character or work habits and influence the way they can approach any job or situation.

76. A: The spokesperson is not included in the interpersonal category of Mintzberg's roles. Interpersonal roles include figurehead, leader, and liaison because the purpose of this category is providing information and managing relationships. Spokesperson is under the informational category because this category includes the roles that process information, and the spokesperson is the representative of their organization.

77. C: The Equal Employment Opportunity Commission (EEOC) is responsible for enforcing Civil Rights Act of 1964, the Equal Pay Act, and the Americans with Disabilities Act, but not the Environmental Protection Act. The EEOC is primarily responsible for enforcing civil rights, while the Environmental Protection Agency (EPA) is responsible for enforcing environmental protection statutes, such as the Clean Air Act or Clean Water Act.

78. A: Marketing refers to all business activities that promote consumer purchases of a business's goods or services. This generally includes researching, identifying, and satisfying consumer needs and wants to the end of making a sale. Organizational behavior is a business discipline that studies how people behave in groups. Other business disciplines include finance, management, and information technology. Communication and sales management are business activities.

79. C: "Bcc" means "blind carbon copy." When an email is sent this way, the recipients do not know who else may be getting it. Sending a cc means that all recipients know who is getting a copy. Forwarding the email or sending a separate email to each recipient would be less time-efficient than a bcc group.

80. D: Owners' equity is comprised of the amount of their initial investment in the business plus any unclaimed profits from the business' operation. (Unclaimed profits are also called retained earnings).

Practice Test #2

1. ABC Toys is a small, independently owned toy store. They are selling the newest doll house on the market for $150. Five miles down the road, Walmart sells the exact same doll house for $120. What is the economic term used to explain why Walmart sells the toy for less than the small toy store?

a. Economies of scale
b. Cost of capital
c. Opportunity cost
d. Price discrimination

2. Each of the following are sentences from a job description. Select the sentence that clearly and correctly communicates its intended meaning.

a. The employee, will have excellent oral communication skills.
b. The employees oral communication skills will be excellent.
c. The employee will communicate orally and in writing well.
d. The employee will have excellent writing skills.

3. Which one of these items is typically recognized as the most important when communicating?

a. Eye contact
b. Spoken words
c. Body language
d. Tone of voice

4. Which of the following is true regarding the subject line in an email?

a. Most people do not bother reading it.
b. It should be just one or two words.
c. It is not necessary on most business emails.
d. It should convey what the message is about.

5. Technological aids can be used to directly fulfill all but which of the following human resources functions?

a. Soliciting resumes for open positions
b. Assessing a new employee's job readiness
c. Communicating information about employee benefits
d. Resolving disputes between employees and management

6. Which goal of business education includes defining a dream job, taking online personality assessments, researching possible careers, and planning which actions to take?

a. Work-based learning
b. Resume preparation
c. Project work
d. Career planning

7. Andrew works in the warehouse of a big box store. As he is stocking shelves, a bolt comes loose, and one of the massive shelving units collapses. Andrew sustains injuries as a result. What form of commercial insurance will cover Andrew's medical expenses and lost wages?

a. Liability insurance
b. Workers' compensation insurance
c. Unemployment compensation insurance
d. Property insurance

8. Which federal agency is responsible for the protection of job applicants or employees from discrimination because of the person's race, color, religion, sex (including pregnancy, gender identity, and sexual orientation), national origin, age (40 or older), disability or genetic information?

a. Occupational Safety and Health Administration
b. Equal Employment Opportunity Commission
c. United States Department of Labor
d. National Labor Relations Board

9. Dividing a broad customer base into different subgroups is referred to as

a. Differentiation
b. Targeting
c. Market segmentation
d. Profiling

10. The main function of a human resources department is to:

a. Meet the company's recruiting goals.
b. Maximize employee productivity while minimizing pay.
c. Facilitate communication between the employer and the employees.
d. Prevent lawsuits.

11. Which would be considered a disadvantage of using the internet for research?

a. Paid advertisements on websites
b. Unknown author credentials
c. Search engine competition
d. Access to information worldwide

12. Effective strategies to recruit students for business education extracurricular activities include the following EXCEPT

a. Giving students extra class credit for participating in these activities
b. Keeping guidance counselors up to date on events, guest speakers, and off-campus activities
c. Using social media for reminders and to post viral videos
d. Offering freebies to new members

13. An individual who is about to retire and wants to earn interest without risking his or her principal would most likely be advised to invest in:

a. Value stocks
b. An S&P 500 index fund
c. A stock-based mutual fund
d. US Treasury bonds

14. What journal entries are made when insurance payable (an accrued expense) is paid?

a. Debit insurance payable; credit cash
b. Credit insurance payable; debit cash
c. Debit insurance expense; credit insurance payable
d. Credit insurance expense; debit insurance payable

15. Professional teacher organizations provide important support to professional educators. What is the largest professional organization designed to promote business education in schools while supporting business education teachers?

a. Association for the Advancement of Computing in Education
b. American Federation of Teachers
c. National Business Education Association
d. International Society for Technology in Education

16. Which type of jurisdiction refers to a court's authority to hear only specific types of cases?

a. Diversity jurisdiction
b. Subject-matter jurisdiction
c. Personal jurisdiction
d. Territorial jurisdiction

17. A company is considering manufacturing a product in several different emerging markets. Which of the following is LEAST likely to influence the company's decision?

a. Likelihood of political instability
b. Labor costs and regulations
c. Cost of shipping goods from that country to the destination country
d. Housing markets in the local area

18. The cluster of shared values, practices, and beliefs of a company is referred to as its

a. Job environment
b. Company culture
c. Selection process
d. Transformation

19. You are teaching a web design course and are preparing a lesson on RGB colors. The art teacher recently taught a lesson on contrasting and complementary colors and has offered to share the materials from that lesson. By using the art teacher's suggestions, your students will have a better understanding of why developers use certain color combinations and avoid others. Simultaneously, the art teacher decides to teach a lesson on color interpretation and screen variances, using some of the material you are discussing in web design. Combining concepts from both web design and art, which type of teaching strategy are you using?

a. Team teaching
b. Cross-curricular instruction
c. Cooperative learning
d. Differentiated instruction

20. An employee reaches out to technical support, and you are the technician who is assigned to the ticket. The employee explains that she needs to locate an important document on her computer for a client, but she cannot find it. You look at her computer and the first thing you notice is that her desktop is cluttered with individual and random files. After doing a search and locating the missing file, what would be your suggestion to her to prevent losing files going forward?

a. Using cloud storage
b. Downloading a file storage program
c. Storing all files on an external hard drive
d. Implementing a file management system

21. Which of the following file types would be best for exporting a document containing text, that is not intended to be changed or copied from in the future?

a. PDF
b. XLSM
c. DOCX
d. JPEG

22. Read the following email and choose which of the following workplace rules the employee neglected to follow.

> To: All Corporate Staff
> From: Gloria Edwards
>
> Subject: [blank]
>
> Hello,
>
> I noticed that someone neglected to refill the coffee pot, AGAIN. I do not know why it is so difficult, and I am tired of being the only person to do anything about it. This needs to be rectified immediately or I am going to start reporting names to management.
>
> Sincerely,
> Gloria

a. Security breach
b. Unauthorized solicitation
c. Network use
d. Netiquette

23. Which of the following terms best describes a situation where an individual enters into an agreement with a company to use the company's business model within a given territory, usually in exchange for a fee?

a. Sole proprietorship
b. Limited liability company
c. Franchise
d. Incorporation

24. Which of the following should be AVOIDED in an oral presentation?

a. Being positive
b. Reading from notes
c. Using visual aids
d. Involving the audience

25. What is the statistical method used to determine the range of acceptable outcomes, based on observable data, to determine the reliability of an estimate? For example, a company needs to create a budget based on the highest and lowest possible revenues and expenses, as they cannot forecast exact numbers with 100% accuracy. Using this method, a business can determine an acceptable range to make financial decisions, knowing their highest and lowest limits.

a. Confidence intervals
b. Probability
c. Coefficient of correlation
d. Standard error of estimate

26. Which term refers to violating copyright-protected software?

a. Copyright theft
b. Internet sharing
c. Software piracy
d. Software patent violation

27. In preparation for a class project, the teacher is discussing computer databases. Which statement should be excluded?

a. Research databases offer collections of related information.
b. Databases include references and citations.
c. Databases are specific in nature.
d. Publishers check the content of databases so the information is more accurate and reliable than general internet searches.

28. If a stock has a high P/E ratio, this means that:

a. The stock's price is low considering the value of the company's earnings
b. The stock pays a high dividend based on its earnings per share
c. The stock's price is high considering the value of its earnings per share
d. The company's earnings per share are high

29. A command economy is characterized by:

a. A laissez-faire approach by the government
b. A moderate amount of government intervention in the economy
c. Businesses commanding all aspects of the economy
d. The government controlling prices and production

30. Which of the following activities provides the best example of collaboration between business education teachers and teachers of other subject areas?

a. Students in a business education class are asked to use their English skills to write cover letters and resumes.
b. Students in a business education class read scientific case studies about research and development for new products.
c. A business education teacher and a math teacher coordinate their lesson plans so that the concepts taught in math class are subsequently applied to real situations in the business class.
d. Students in a business class learn to balance checkbooks after watching a video lesson from a mathematics professor.

31. Emily is enrolled in a career development course at her high school. Her final project in the course is to complete a career portfolio consisting of several elements, such as a cover letter, resume, and an essay detailing "A Day in the Life of ____," based on the career she has chosen. Emily thinks she wants to pursue a career in accounting, like her mother, but does not know if she would enjoy that career for the rest of her life. As her teacher, what would you advise Emily to do to gain a better understanding of what a day in the life of an accountant is like?

a. Ask her mother's opinion.
b. Shadow an accountant.
c. Research accounting as a career.
d. Visit colleges offering accounting degrees.

32. Which of these tasks would NOT be a primary function of an organization's human resources department?

a. Recruiting, screening, and training new employees
b. Managing employee benefits
c. Managing client accounts
d. Coordinating payroll activities

33. In the classroom, the business education teacher has paired students to conduct mock job interviews. Students take turns being the interviewer and the applicant. Which pedagogical technique is being used?

a. Student-centered learning
b. Socratic method
c. Role play
d. Project work

34. Of the following, which is an advantage of using analytical checklists for assessment?

a. They allow for differences in assessing individual tasks across students.
b. They require additional notes to identify other notable feats observed.
c. They save time and effort by listing tasks, skills, or behaviors in advance.
d. They sometimes constrain assessment to Yes/No without quality levels.

35. Which of these steps in the accounting cycle comes first?

a. Prepare an unadjusted trial balance.
b. Identify relevant transactions.
c. Create financial statements.
d. Record transactions in a journal.

36. Which of the following would generally NOT be an example of an eligible leave under the Family and Medical Leave Act (FMLA)?

a. A child is being placed with the employee for foster care.
b. An employee's mother-in-law becomes seriously ill.
c. An employee gives birth to a child.
d. The spouse of an employee develops a serious health condition.

37. Joe is a highly skilled baker working for a large bakery in the city. Joe does not believe his skills are being recognized and he doesn't like reporting to anyone else. Joe has decided to open a bakery in his town. However, he does not have enough initial capital to start a business on his own. His brother, Steve, has offered to lend enough cash to get Joe started up, but has no interest in running a bakery. What is the most likely type of business structure for the bakery?

a. Partnership
b. Sole proprietorship
c. Joint venture
d. Limited liability company

38. What is the name of the field concerned with increasing productivity while minimizing discomfort and risk of injury?

a. User-friendly efficiency
b. Comfort design
c. Ergonomics
d. Structural design

39. Mrs. Eli is holding a career day for her fifth-grade class of 25 students, and she has invited parents to come to class and discuss their jobs. Many parents have expressed interest, but most of them have said that they will have difficulty leaving their jobs during the school day. Which of the following technological solutions might be the least helpful in addressing this problem?

a. Holding the presentation by video conference during the parents' lunch breaks
b. Holding the presentation by teleconference during the parents' lunch breaks
c. Asking the parents to create a videotape in which they discuss their job and send it to school
d. Asking the parents to create a slide show presentation about their job for their child to present to the class

40. Which of the following examples demonstrates a conflict between verbal and nonverbal communication?

a. A sales representative does a presentation to a potential client, making eye contact, speaking in a clear and even tone, and using hand gestures occasionally to accentuate an important point.
b. A candidate for an open position arrives to an interview dressed in a business suit, makes eye contact with the hiring manager, shakes hands with the interviewer, and speaks confidently.
c. A vendor arrives at a business to negotiate a contract. The vendor representative smiles often, speaks clearly and confidently, and maintains good posture, even during tense moments.
d. An employee meets with her manager to discuss a rumor she heard about layoffs. As he looks down at his computer, the manager says in a high-pitched voice not to be concerned because the rumors are false.

41. In the international business environment, which factor includes changes in tax rates and foreign trade regulations?

a. Cultural
b. Economic
c. Legal
d. Political

42. A business education teacher teaches two classes of 30 9th graders during a semester. At the end of the class, students are given identical tests on the course material. Students in Class 1, which was taught using a traditional lecture approach, scored an average of 73% on the test. Students in Class 2, which was taught using interactive exercises and computer-based simulations, scored an average of 82% on the test. What can be concluded from this experiment?

a. The students in Class 2 are more intelligent than those in Class 1.
b. The teaching methods used for Class 2 are superior to those used for Class 1.
c. Nothing can be concluded from these results because one semester is not a long enough period of time to accurately measure learning.
d. Nothing can be concluded from these results because students' baseline performance on these tests was not measured before the experiment.

43. Which teaching method for business education involves analyzing a historical event in order to learn from real-life situations?

a. Lectures
b. Case study
c. Skill practice
d. Research

44. In order to start an online business, an individual would need all but which of the following:

a. A business model
b. A website
c. An email address
d. A printer

45. Which of the following is MOST directly related to a weaker US dollar?

a. Foreign exports increase
b. US exports increase
c. Foreign exports decrease
d. US exports decrease

46. What is true about an effective instructional strategy that improves teaching effectiveness and student performance

a. Teachers' telling students success stories will not help them see cause and effect.
b. Teachers should have students keep logs to help them connect efforts to results.
c. Teachers' tangible rewards to students are more effective than symbolic rewards.
d. Teachers should ensure equitable treatment by making student rewards uniform.

47. Ms. Tomkins is a third-grade teacher. This school year, her class is unusually large. The district is unable to hire another third-grade teacher, so they have assigned the enrichment teacher, Mrs. Smith, to assist her class. Mrs. Smith has many years of experience with students who need extra support. The teachers decide that they will teach the same material but will break the students into two groups for reading and math lessons. Mrs. Smith will work with a small group of students who need more guidance, and Ms. Tomkins will instruct the remaining students. What form of co-teaching is happening in this classroom?

a. Team teaching
b. Alternative teaching
c. Station teaching
d. Parallel teaching

48. Which of these objectives of business education refers to being job-ready?

a. Learning academic skills in core areas
b. Understanding emerging technologies
c. Learning American business operations
d. Learning employability skills

49. What type of business is the most common employer of high-school students?

a. Grocery stores
b. Movie theaters
c. Clothing stores
d. Restaurants

50. In 1979, the nuclear reactor facility at Three Mile Island experienced the worst commercial nuclear power plant disaster in US history. Appropriate safety controls and procedures were lacking, and human error worsened the situation due to lack of adequate training. The result was a partial meltdown which emitted radioactive gases. Which common management process would have likely prevented this disaster?

a. Regulatory standards
b. Project management
c. Automation
d. Quality control

51. Which of the following constitutes the most defensible binding contract?

a. An agreement signed and dated by one party and one witness
b. An agreement signed and dated by both parties
c. An agreement signed by both parties and witnessed by a third party
d. An agreement signed and dated by both parties and a witness

52. Which financial report is considered a "snapshot" of one moment in time?

a. Income statement
b. Cash flow statement
c. Balance sheet
d. Statement of changes in owner's equity

53. Linda is a 75-year-old woman. She is cautious with her finances and always pays her bills on time. Linda recently received a phone call from a person identifying themselves as a representative of her banking institution. This individual told Linda that she had defaulted on a loan and that she would need to pay the $10,000 on the balance of her loan immediately, or she would be arrested for fraud. In a panic, Linda gave the caller permission to access her bank account, including the username and password for her online banking. The caller was a fraud and stole Linda's life savings. What type of scam did Linda fall prey to?

a. Bait and switch
b. Phishing
c. Identity theft
d. Cramming

54. When researching a presentation about a national shipping business, the most detailed and comprehensive source of information about the top management of the company and its competitors would most likely be:

a. The company's investor-relations website
b. Hoovers.com
c. LexisNexis.com
d. The catalogue at your local library

55. What is the primary function of the notes panel when in the presentation mode of a slideshow?

a. To provide a place to take notes when listening to the presentation
b. To provide the author a space to pause and refine his presentation while in a timed rehearsal
c. To provide the presenter with text that is hidden from the audience
d. To provide the presenter with a preview of the next slide before switching

56. Which of the following countries is not part of the USMCA?

a. Mexico
b. United States
c. Canada
d. China

57. Which of the following applications is best suited to store information about a classroom that includes the students, their attendance, and their grades and that will be able to generate formatted reports showing their attendance and grade progress?

a. A spreadsheet software
b. A presentation software
c. A database management system
d. A word processor

58. Corporate investors rely on data from the ____ to determine the creditworthiness and financial health of a company.

a. stock market
b. chief financial officer (CFO)
c. financial statements
d. Securities and Exchange Commission

59. Which term refers to the amount that a country's cost of imports exceeds its exports?

a. Trade balance
b. Trade deficit
c. Trade surplus
d. Trade dollars

60. A human resources manager is likely to be responsible for all but which of the following:

a. Sales
b. Payroll
c. Hiring
d. Training

61. How is the current ratio (an indicator of liquidity) calculated?

a. Current liabilities divided by current assets
b. Current assets divided by current liabilities
c. Current assets multiplied by current liabilities
d. Current assets minus current liabilities

62. A manufacturing company implements anti-pollution measures outlined by applicable legislation but opts not to adopt any additional anti-pollution measures. This company has most likely adopted which of the following approaches to business-society relations?

a. Social Responsiveness Approach
b. Social Responsibility Approach
c. Social Obligation Approach
d. Cost-benefit Approach

63. What is the primary difference between coaching and mentoring?

a. Coaching is generally used for a specific reason—either to prepare an individual for a new challenge or to change a specific work behavior.
b. Coaching is generally conducted in a one-on-one setting.
c. Coaching is usually used in the case of pending, or as a result of, disciplinary action.
d. Coaching is more focused on instructional job training, while mentoring focuses on personal goals and aspirations.

64. When developing a strategic plan, in which section would the business show the results of a SWOT analysis?

a. Situation analysis
b. Goal setting
c. Evaluation
d. Strategy implementation

65. Which is NOT true of the Strengthening Career and Technical Education for the 21st Century Act (Perkins V)?

a. Its objective is to improve technical education in all 50 states.
b. There are requirements to connect academic content with technical education.
c. Funding is not dependent on annual Congressional approval.
d. The amended law guaranteed funding through 2024.

66. Which of the following best explains how political instability can affect economic growth?

a. Investors get nervous and are more conservative with their investments.
b. Business owners are reluctant to invest capital.
c. Consumers spend less, resulting in an increase in supply and decrease in demand.
d. Uncertainty in government regulation results in a halt in production.

67. Which of the following is an advantage of using anecdotal notes to assess student work?

a. Teachers can use these to collect information both during assessment and outside of it.
b. Unless a teacher adds norms or criteria for comparison, these notes lack standardization.
c. Teachers cannot record observations of individual student behaviors as with most tools.
d. Writing anecdotal notes can yield valuable insights but often lacks any supporting context.

68. Which of the following would best qualify as a secure password?

a. Your birthdate
b. A random string of letters and numbers
c. A word followed by a three-digit number
d. A word with a few letters changed to symbols of similar appearance

69. Which of the following is NOT an effective approach for a supervisor delivering feedback to a struggling employee?

a. The supervisor should list every area of deficiency and how it impacts the team and/or organization.
b. The supervisor should provide specific examples of instances in which the employee had a misstep.
c. The supervisor should make performance expectations clear.
d. The supervisor should provide some praise around the things the employee is performing well.

70. Which of the following questions would NOT potentially be illegal to ask a job candidate at a pre-employment interview?

a. Have you ever requested workers' compensation benefits?
b. Do you have any disabilities that would interfere with your ability to perform this job?
c. What are you salary expectations?
d. What will you do for childcare if you get the job?

71. Anna is interested in purchasing a computer for her small landscaping business. She wants to be able to compose simple fliers and advertising materials, communicate with clients via email, and order supplies online. Which of the following lists best describes the hardware and software components that Anna's computer should look for?

a. An internet connection, Quickbooks, and at least 16 GB of memory
b. An internet connection, word processing software, and Quickbooks
c. An internet connection, word processing software, and 8 GB of memory
d. An internet connection, Quickbooks, and 8 GB of memory

72. The specific choices businesses make when bringing their goods and services to the market are referred to as ____________________

a. strategic planning
b. marketing oversight
c. targeting consumers
d. marketing mix

73. Which of the following interview practice are job applicants generally NOT recommended to employ?

a. Researching the company beforehand
b. Turning weaknesses into strengths
c. Asking about salary and benefits
d. Following up immediately to show interest

74. What is the communication style where the individual asks for what is needed, says what is felt, and is respectful of others?

a. Passive
b. Aggressive
c. Assertive
d. Visual

75. Which management style is the least controlling?

a. Laissez-faire
b. Autocratic
c. Democratic
d. Collaborative

Refer to the following for questions 76–77:

Businesses often partner with local schools to offer support in many ways. They may assist with fundraising efforts or may work with individual students with job shadowing or work study programs. This week, the owner of a local business is coming into a business education classroom to conduct mock job interviews with students. She wants to help students learn how to discuss non-technical skills that include flexibility, teamwork, and time management.

76. What is the common term used to describe a business's involvement in its community?

a. Social responsibility
b. Corporate citizenship
c. Public relations
d. Due diligence

77. What are the skills that the business owner wants to teach students called?

a. Hard skills
b. Requisite skills
c. Personality skills
d. Soft skills

78. Assuming supply remains the same (no increase or decrease), what is the impact of an increase in demand on the equilibrium price?

a. The equilibrium price will increase
b. The equilibrium price will decrease
c. The equilibrium price will remain the same
d. Shifts in demand do not impact the equilibrium price

79. What term is used to describe the process of starting a new business and operating it to generate a profit?

a. Job creation
b. GDP growth
c. Venture capital
d. Entrepreneurship

80. Which of the following is the best description of intranet?

a. A portion of the World Wide Web used as a private internet network.
b. An offline version of the internet used for testing new web pages prior to making them live.
c. A virtual private network (VPN), where an authorized user may remotely access files in a private network.
d. A local network where a company can share files, which is restricted from public use.

Answer Key and Explanations for Test #2

1. A: Walmart can purchase a very large quantity of doll houses which will be sold by their stores nationwide. This gives them leverage to negotiate a better price with the manufacturer. ABC Toys will only order a few doll houses, so the manufacturer does not have incentive to offer them the same deal they offered to Walmart. In this example, Walmart is benefiting from the economic concept of economies of scale.

2. D: "The employee will have excellent writing skills" states the desired qualification clearly and correctly. "The employee, will have excellent oral communication skills" is incorrect because the comma is unnecessary. In the second sentence, "employees" is meant to be possessive, and should have an apostrophe ("employee's"). The second sentence is also written in passive language, which is not technically incorrect, but may convey a lack of clarity. In the third sentence, the word "well" is misplaced and would be best placed next to the verb which it modifies ("communicate well" would be correct).

3. C: According to a study by UCLA Professor Emeritus Albert Mehrabian, body language contributes 55 percent to a conversation, followed by tone of voice (38 percent) and spoken words (7 percent). Lessons on effective business communication should include appropriate body language.

4. D: A subject line is an important part of an email and should contain a strong clue about what the message is about.

5. D: Technological aids such as email and computer software programs can be used to directly fulfill human resources functions like soliciting resumes for open positions, assessing a new employee's job readiness, or communicating information about employee benefits; however, a complicated situation such as an employee-employer dispute requires listening and negotiation skills and judgment that cannot be replaced by a computer.

6. D: Career planning and development involves setting short-, medium-, and long-term goals. Business education classes include strategies and tools to be used for career planning, which includes resume preparation. Project work refers to group learning activities. Work-based learning refers to business-school partnerships.

7. B: Workers' compensation insurance is required in most states. It covers employees who may have a work-related illness or injury. Workers' compensation covers medical expenses, lost wages, and even covers the company if the employee files a lawsuit in some instances.

8. B: While all of these agencies protect individuals in the workplace, the Equal Employment Opportunity Commission (EEOC) is the primary federal agency responsible for protection against discrimination. The EEOC has the authority to investigate reports of discrimination and can even sue the company if they are able to determine an individual has been discriminated against.

9. C: Market segmentation allows companies to personalize marketing campaigns, which leads to a more efficient use of marketing resources. These target markets allow businesses to focus on common demographics (e.g., hurricane-reinforced windows might be marketed to those who live in areas prone to tropical storms).

10. C: The main function of a human resources department is to facilitate communication between the employer and the employees. While human resources departments are primarily responsible to the company's upper management, they are intended to provide a "neutral" conduit through which personnel policies can be devised and implemented and through which employees can express and resolve concerns.

11. B: Internet research offers many advantages over traditional library or database research. In addition to providing immediate access to free resources, search results include message boards, blogs, and related information. One of the few disadvantages is that not all information comes from credible sources, and the authorship can be unclear. When using internet sources, fact checking and corroboration of information is essential. It is usually a best practice to rely only on peer-reviewed and academic sources, rather than sources that are publicly controlled. Other disadvantages of internet sources include misinformation, information overload, and a lack of organized results.

12. A: Sharing information online about the value of these activities, having sign-up areas during lunch and before school, using social media, keeping guidance counselors up to date on events, and offering freebies to new members are all effective strategies to educate students about the benefits of business education. Most school districts prohibit extra credit for assignments that are not directly connected to the curriculum or state standards.

13. D: An individual who is about to retire and wants to earn interest without risking his or her principal would most likely be advised to invest in US Treasury bonds. Value stocks, S&P 500 index funds, and stock-based mutual funds are all tied to the stock market, which is far more volatile and risky than US Treasury bonds. Some other bond investments, like junk bonds, can be quite risky. Since this investor is more concerned with protecting the principal than with earning high returns, an investment in bonds would best match his or her objective.

14. A: When an expense is incurred but not paid, journal entries reflect the expense on the income statement and the current liability on the balance sheet. When payment is made, the liability is removed, and cash or a different current asset (e.g., bank account) is reduced.

15. C: The National Business Education Association is the "nation's leading professional organization devoted exclusively to serving individuals and groups engaged in instruction, administration, research, and dissemination of information for and about business." (Citation: https://nbea.org/default.aspx) The NBEA helps teachers with professional development opportunities. They also work to promote business education programs and improve existing programs.

16. B: Subject-matter jurisdiction includes bankruptcy, probate, juvenile, family law, and small claims courts. Only cases specific to these matters can be tried in these courts. Personal jurisdiction concerns an individual (e.g., a resident of a specific state); and territorial jurisdiction refers to events that happened in an area under the court's jurisdiction.

17. D: Housing markets may play some role in establishing new businesses and looking for factors that directly influence employee stability, but it is less likely to influence whether or not to manufacture a product for specific markets. Political instability could put the company's investment at risk, and the labor and shipping costs associated with a given country can be a decisive factor in investment decisions.

18. B: Company culture is a set of shared values and goals that is reflected in decision-making, conflict resolution, and employee interactions. It is also present in hiring practices, so prospective employees should seek to determine if they will be comfortable in the established company culture.

19. B: This is an example of cross-curricular learning. This collaboration between teachers of different subjects allows students to apply what they learn in one class to another. This is beneficial to students who may be stronger in one subject compared to another. In this example, a student may really enjoy art but may not like learning about web design. Bringing in art elements can make the lesson more engaging for those students. Conversely, some students may have strong technology skills but may not enjoy art as much.

20. D: This employee needs to implement a file management system to organize her files to prevent losing them again. Sorting her files into similar topics or functions and creating folders to store them will help her locate what she needs much faster next time.

21. A: Portable Document Format (PDF) is commonly used for displaying different types of content, and can be used to encrypt and lock elements to deter change or theft. The format .docx could be used to prevent alteration, but it does not prevent readers from copying and pasting content into new documents.

22. D: This is an example of poor netiquette. Netiquette is the term used to describe the appropriate way to communicate electronically. In this example, Gloria used a company email group to reach out to the entire staff of the company, likely including upper management of the company. This is not a good use of anyone's time or of company assets. While Gloria may be right in her statement, her method does not justify her actions.

23. C: When an individual enters into an agreement with a company to use the company's business model within a given territory, this is called a franchise agreement. In most cases, the individual pays the company a franchise fee, usually a percentage of gross revenue, in order to use the company's business model.

24. B: You should never read from notes when giving an oral presentation unless absolutely necessary, which is rare (except in work situations). Reading from notes not only bores the audience, which means that you're on the verge of losing their focused attention, it also insults them. When you have to read from prepared notes, you send the message to your audience that either they're not important enough to cause you to take the time to work on your speech or that your message isn't important enough to cause you to prepare properly.

25. A: The confidence interval helps businesses assess the reliability of an estimate based on data gathered from previous sales, historical expenses, customer information, etc. Because an estimate may not be 100% accurate, the confidence interval provides a range of acceptable outcomes, allowing for a small margin of error or adjustment.

26. C: Software piracy is the unauthorized use of protected software and is also known as copyright infringement. The most common software piracy involves counterfeiting (the illegal use, copying, or selling of protected work). Other examples of copyright infringement include recording movies in a theater, downloading music illegally, and reselling digital files.

27. C: In addition to offering collections of related information with bibliographies and citations, databases are checked by publishers to ensure their content is accurate and reliable. Databases can be specific or general in nature.

28. C: If a stock has a high P/E ratio, this means that the stock's price is high considering the value of its earnings per share (EPS). The P/E ratio is calculated by dividing the share price by the company's EPS. The closer the result is to zero, the cheaper the stock is in relation to the amount of money the company is earning.

29. D: A command economy (also known as a planned economy) is characterized by the government controlling nearly all aspects of the economy, including prices and production. This type of economy is traditionally associated with Communist economies where prices, wages and production quotas are set by the government. A, B, and C are all incorrect because they imply some form of private sector autonomy.

30. C: A business education teacher and a math teacher coordinating their lesson plans so that the concepts taught in math class are subsequently applied to real situations in the business class is the best example of interdisciplinary collaboration. While the other examples do require students to use skills learned in other classes like math and language arts, only example C involves active coordination between teachers in two different subject areas.

31. B: Emily's best bet is to participate in a job shadowing experience. This would allow her to experience an actual day in the life of an accountant. While interviewing her mom and asking her opinion can be helpful, it would not give her a thorough understanding of what it would feel like to work in that industry every day. The same is true of career research and visiting colleges; Emily could learn as much about the career as possible, but without experiencing it hands-on, she would not know for certain if that career is a good match for her.

32. C: Recruiting, screening, and training job applicants; managing employee benefits; and coordinating payroll activities are functions of the human resources department. Staffing and development as well as employee and labor relations also fall under the human resources umbrella.

33. C: Role play allows students to practice real-life scenarios by interacting with others. The experience and relevant feedback will prepare them for the actual situations. The Socratic method requires critical thinking skills to answer questions in a cooperative (although argumentative) format. Student-centered learning shifts the classroom focus from teacher-directed activities to the learners. Think-pair-share and project work are also collaborative practices.

34. C: Using analytical checklists as assessment tools has the advantage of saving time and effort by listing the tasks, skills, or behaviors to be performed and assessed in advance. They also have the advantage of making assessment uniform across students relative to tasks and/or their components, making choice A incorrect. They do require additional notes for teachers to identify other notable feats that teachers observe students accomplishing beyond the designated tasks (B), but this is a disadvantage. Although some checklists include performance levels similarly to rubrics, others constrain assessment to Yes/No responses (D), another disadvantage.

35. B: The first step of the accounting cycle is to identify all relevant transactions that are considered bookkeeping events. These include (but are not limited to) sales, refunds, and payments to employees or vendors. Transactions are recorded using journal entries and then posted to a general ledger. Preparing an unadjusted trial balance and creating a worksheet allow for a review before adjusting entries are made. Financial statements are then created, and the books are closed.

36. B: The Family and Medical Leave Act (FMLA) protects the jobs of employees in companies with at least 50 employees in the event of certain illnesses or family needs. This leave is usually unpaid and does not guarantee the employee will have the same job when they return. This usually only covers the employee and their immediate family members, which does not include the employee's in-laws.

37. B: The most likely form of business structure would be a sole proprietorship. Joe wants to run his own business and only be accountable to himself. Steve wants to help his brother but does not have any interest in running a bakery. In this situation, Joe would start a sole proprietorship and

Steve would be an unofficial investor. Sole prorietorships cannot have investors in the traditional sense, but a sole proprietor may take a loan from an entity or a person. A partnership would exist if Steve wanted to help with the management and operating of the bakery. A joint venture is a newly formed enterprise by two or more separate businesses for a special project or a new business. A limited liability company (LLC) is a partnership that has gone through the steps of filing articles of organization, which separates the owners from personal liability.

38. C: Fundamental principles of ergonomics include keeping everything within reach, maintaining proper posture, minimizing excessive motion, and reducing fatigue. The basic premise is to fit the environment to the person. Desk chairs are a good example of this, as they are used for long periods of time and help to maintain good posture for computer use. To compare, lawn chairs are not made to be sat in every day for long periods of time. Their function is more centered on portability and cost effectiveness, rather than comfort or safety.

39. B: A video conference could be arranged so all of the students can easily see the parent and the parent can see the students and respond to their questions, and slide show or videotaping would also be effective at conveying the information if video conferencing technology was not available. Conducting a teleconference with parents while they're on their lunch breaks would probably not be as effective because it would require students to gather around one speakerphone or each have their own phones.

40. D: Nonverbal communication is often a more accurate portrayal of communication than spoken words. Making eye contact, using hand gestures appropriate to the conversation, and having good posture are all examples of positive nonverbal communication. Avoiding eye contact and speaking with a nervous or high-pitched voice communicate nervousness or dishonesty, even if the words that are spoken seem to indicate otherwise.

41. D: Political factors include government stability, changes in tax rates, and foreign trade regulations. Cultural factors include education, customs, and lifestyle. Economic factors include interest rates, supply and demand, and inflation. Legal factors refer to the country's laws in areas such as age discrimination, minimum wage, and environmental regulations.

42. D: Nothing can be concluded from these results because students' baseline performance on these tests was not measured before the experiment. It is possible that one group of students already knew more about business or were more academically advanced to start with. In order to account for this possibility, each group of students should have been tested prior to the beginning of the class. The effectiveness of the two teaching methods could then be compared based on the change in students' scores between the first and second test administrations.

43. B: Case studies employ research strategies to analyze real-life scenarios. Lectures, group work, research, work-based experience, and skill practice (e.g., keyboarding) are also effective teaching methods.

44. D: In order to start an online business, an individual would need an Internet connection, email, and a web domain, but a printer would not necessarily be required, since documents can be scanned and sent via email.

45. B: When US dollar or products are less expensive for foreign customers, then US firms will export more products. If US products are more expensive for foreign customers, then US firms will export fewer products. The amount of exporting done by foreign nations is not necessarily affected by the US exchange rate.

46. B: As educator expert Robert Marzano has noted, effective instructional strategies include relating success stories to students, which reinforces their efforts in school and helps them see the causal relationship between effort and achievement. Another strategy that promotes this connection is having students keep logs and analyze them (B). Marzano advises teachers to give symbolic, not tangible, rewards to students (C) to recognize their efforts and achievements more effectively, and to personalize or individualize those rewards for each student to make them more meaningful and relevant than uniform rewards (D).

47. B: These two teachers are participating in alternative teaching. This strategy involves one teacher working with a small group of students requiring specialized attention, while the other teacher is responsible for the larger group of students. This reduces the number of students Ms. Tomkins must instruct overall, and it provides additional support to those students who may otherwise not receive the attention they need. Team teaching involves both teachers delivering instruction simultaneously. Station teaching divides students into several groups and divides content, with each teacher working at a different station. Parallel teaching is similar to alternative teaching, except students are divided evenly rather than by need.

48. D: Employability skills (also referred to as workplace readiness) are significant because they show employers that students have academic skills in core areas (math, reading, critical thinking) and the appropriate communication and personality skills for the workplace. Employability skills are taught throughout secondary education curriculum. Business education also includes learning employability skills through personality and career assessments, reviewing post-secondary options, and the skills necessary during the job application process (preparing resumes and cover letters, practicing interviews, communicating with companies) to be job ready.

49. D: Restaurants are the most common employer of high-school students, based on data from the United States Bureau of Labor Statistics. These students will have direct experience with the cost of food, as well as with the nutritional choices available in a restaurant.

50. D: A quality control process would likely have prevented this disaster, or at least reduced its effects on the environment. Mechanical controls should have been in place, as well as a system of routine safety procedures. Human error could also have been prevented if employees were properly trained to prevent situations like this from arising and taught what to do about them if problems happen.

51. D: A binding contract is any agreement, whether verbal or written, and it does not have to be signed, dated, or witnessed to be valid. However, despite the legality of a "hand-shake" agreement, a contract is most defensible legally when there is evidence that can be demonstrated if a party does not abide by the terms of the agreement. The most defensible contract would be one that has multiple types of evidence that can paint a picture of who was involved, what the agreement was in detail, when the agreement took place, and a witness who can unbiasedly attest to the details of the arrangement.

52. C: The balance sheet reports the entity's assets, liabilities, and owner's equity at a specific moment. A balance sheet's title includes the date and may include the phrase "as of _____." The other three reports present information covering a period of time that is also specified in the report's title.

53. B: Linda was a victim of a phishing scam. The culprit was posing as an official of her trusted banking institution, using her trust and fear to scare her into giving her personal information to the scammer.

54. B: When researching a presentation about a national shipping business, the most detailed and comprehensive source of information about the top management of the company and its competitors would most likely be Hoovers.com. LexisNexis.com is also useful for business research, but it is a searchable database of academic and news articles, rather than a database of information about specific companies and industries, like Hoovers. The local newspaper or library would be unlikely to have detailed information about competitors across the country, although it may have specific information about those located in the immediate vicinity. The company's investor-relations website is unlikely to have the type of information publicly available for the person in question.

55. C: The notes panel is used to write hidden notes about what to say when presenting. This panel can be useful in developing a more refined presentation and can be printed to provide the audience if desired. It is not displayed on the presentation screen when projected.

56. D: China is not part of the USMCA. THE USMCA refers to the United States-Mexico-Canada Agreement, which is an agreement implemented in 2020 to encourage trade between the US, Canada, and Mexico.

57. C: A database management system can store data, retrieve it, and display the data with complex reports for printing or online use. Spreadsheets can be used to perform various complex calculations with numbers and charts. While spreadsheets can be useful for tracking smaller amounts of data and performing calculations, they are not as suitable for larger data sets (like student records). Presentation software is generally used to create slide shows and display audio and visual presentations. Word processors can create simple documents like memos or more complex, formatted technical writing.

58. C: Investors need to determine the current and potential future success of a company in order to see a return on investment. Financial statements document the assets, liabilities, equity, revenues and expenses, net income/loss, and liquidity of current assets of the company. This information is essential for investors to make profitable decisions.

59. B: Trade balance, or balance of trade, is a measurement of a country's economic strength and is calculated as the difference between its imports and its exports. A trade deficit (also called a negative balance of trade) is the amount that a country's imports exceed its exports. A trade surplus is just the opposite—the amount that a country's exports exceed its imports. Trade dollars were silver coins used to facilitate trade with the Far East in the 1800s.

60. A: A human resources manager is likely to be responsible for hiring, training, and payroll, but not sales. Human resources managers are in charge of employer-employee relations, including any activity that involves recruiting and retaining valuable employees.

61. B: Current assets include cash and other assets that can be turned into cash within a year (e.g., inventory, CDs held in banks). Current liabilities are obligations due within a year. The current ratio indicates an entity's ability to pay short-term obligations. Depending on the industry, a current ratio (sometimes referred to as a working capital ratio) of 1.00 is considered good. Working capital is calculated as current assets minus current liabilities and is a different formula used to determine the funds available for day-to-day operations.

62. C: A manufacturing company that implements anti-pollution measures as outlined by applicable legislation but opts not to introduce any additional anti-pollution measures has most likely adopted the Social Obligation Approach to business-society relations. This means that the business will follow all applicable laws but will not make any supplemental attempts to improve the environment or contribute to social welfare. This model is based upon cost-benefit calculations, but such calculations are not an approach to business-society relations in and of themselves. The Social Responsibility and Social Responsiveness approaches denote moderate and high levels of social involvement, respectively.

63. A: Coaching is used in specific instances for individuals—to help them prepare for a leadership role or an upcoming assignment or to help them develop a specific skill or stop exhibiting a certain behavior. Mentoring is usually in the case of a formal or informal program and can help individuals pursue their personal or professional goals.

64. A: A SWOT analysis is outlined in the situation analysis section of the strategic plan. This demonstrates the business's strengths, weaknesses, opportunities, and threats. This section is devoted to analyzing the internal functions of the business, as well as the industry in which the business operates.

65. C: Perkins V funding is provided through annual congressional appropriations (it is not guaranteed in advance); the statute authorized appropriations through FY2019–FY2024. This law encourages states and local leaders to develop new options for career and technical education, and it includes requirements to connect academic content with technical education. The most recent reauthorization (2018) changed the term from "vocational education" to "career and technical education."

66. A: Investors will only invest if they are certain of a return on their investment. Ever-changing government policy and political unrest makes it difficult for investors to be confident. Less investment means less capital to invest in business, resulting in less output and limited economic growth.

67. A: One advantage of writing anecdotal notes as an assessment tool is that teachers can collect information about student skills and behaviors outside of assessment activities as well as during them; this can help teachers realize valuable insights into student learning and behavior. The fact that such notes are not standardized unless the teacher incorporates norms or criteria for comparison (B) is a disadvantage. An advantage of anecdotal notes is that teachers *can* record observations of individual student behaviors, which standard test instruments, checklists, and most other tools do *not* allow (C). The fact that anecdotal notes often lack any supporting context (D) is a disadvantage.

68. B: A secure password should be difficult for malicious hackers to guess, or to arrive at by any sort of automated process. Your birthdate is a very poor password, since it's not hard for other people to find out, and because many people have used birthdates as passwords in the past it's something a hacker would be likely to try. Dictionary words also make poor passwords; certainly a hacker is unlikely to manually try every word in the dictionary, but it's not hard to write a program that can do so. Adding a three-digit number to the end of the word, or changing some letters to symbols, helps a little, but not enough; it multiplies the necessary number of guesses by a factor of a thousand or so, but that may still be small enough to be "cracked" by an automated program. On the other hand, the number of possibilities for a random string of letters and numbers is far too large to make it feasible to guess such a password. A typical English dictionary contains a few hundred thousand words, but there are more than two trillion possible eight-digit strings of letters and numbers. Using longer strings, and using symbols as well as letters and numbers, further increases the possibilities and therefore the security.

Of course, while such a password may be very secure, it has the disadvantage of being hard to remember. One way to minimize this issue is to use a password manager that keeps track of difficult-to-remember passwords.

69. A: When providing feedback, a supervisor should limit the focus to one or two areas of deficiency. Otherwise, it tends to make the employee feel defensive.

70. C: It could be illegal to ask questions dictated in options A, B, and D in many states in the US. The Americans with Disabilities Act prohibits employers from attempting to ascertain a prospective employee's disability status prior to hiring the job candidate. Questions A and B could be construed as violations of this act. Questions regarding childcare arrangements can be considered intent to discriminate, thus violating Title VII of the Civil Rights Act. Asking about salary expectations is not illegal.

71. C: Anna would need word processing software, an Internet connection, and a minimum of 8 GB of memory to keep up with basic computing standards. Word processing software would allow Anna to compose simple fliers and advertising materials, and an Internet connection would allow Anna to communicate with clients via email and order supplies online. 8 GB of memory is what standard home and small business computers need, and Quickbooks is a type of accounting software that may be useful for Anna, but would not be necessary for the tasks listed in this question.

72. D: Marketing mix is a model for business marketing centered around product, place, price, and promotion, known collectively as the 4 Ps, which helps the business to determine their particular objectives in business. The tasks of strategic planning, marketing oversight, and targeting consumers may be used in addition to the marketing mix.

73. C: Unless the interviewer asks you directly, your salary and benefits concerns should not be brought up during the initial conversation; however, it is important to research the employer beforehand (both to understand the job and to prepare questions) and follow up immediately with a letter or email. When an interviewer asks about weaknesses, the question can be used as an opportunity to frame shortcomings as strengths by explaining how you have learned from them and gained better skills in the process.

74. C: Being assertive allows the individual to communicate feelings and thoughts while also respecting those of others. Passive communicators seek to avoid making their needs known and often speak softly and apologetically. Those who are aggressive typically have no regard for others and are sometimes considered abusive.

75. A: Management style refers to how managers accomplish objectives and the relationships they have with their subordinates. Laissez-faire relies on the autonomy of expert staff and has little or no management control. Autocratic is the most controlling style and is described as top-down. It includes authoritative and persuasive styles. Democratic style encourages employee input, but the final decision rests with the manager. Collaborative is a democratic style in which the manager seeks employee opinions and believes that implementing the choice of the majority will lead to employee acceptance.

76. B: Corporate citizenship means that businesses need to participate in the communities in which they reside, beyond just paying their local taxes. Partnerships with local school districts are one way they can maintain a good image and relationship in their communities. This is mutually beneficial to the school and the business. Many contributions are tax deductible, reducing or eliminating the expense to the business and improving the school's benefit with the added financial support.

77. D: Soft skills are personal attributes that enable employees to interact. Because of the importance of these skills in the workplace, educators are expected to include lessons on them. Job applicants should include these personality traits in their cover letters and discuss them in job interviews.

78. A: The equilibrium price is the point where supply is equal to the amount of product demanded. It is the price consumers are willing to pay for producers to maintain current supply. When demand increases, the equilibrium price will increase. Conversely, if demand were to decrease, the equilibrium price would also fall.

79. D: Entrepreneurship is the process of starting a new business. Venture capital is the funds invested in a new business by private investors. Job creation and GDP growth are ways that the economy is measured and are not solely related to new businesses.

80. D: Intranet is used by companies who need to network among a limited, usually local, group of users. The access to an intranet is usually restricted to only the staff members of an organization. This type of network is often crucial in information technology management in troubleshooting and assisting employees in handling technology-centered needs.